In and Out
of
Their Elements

To Clark, der ausgezeichnete Schriftsteller, from the Lexington antique, John

In and Out of Their Elements

by

John N. Miller

Fine Tooth Press

This is a collection of poetry. Characters, places, and incidents have been filtered through the author's imagination, and they have been, therefore, inevitably and irrevocably altered and should not be mistaken for reality.

First edition published 2006.

ISBN 13: 978-0-9766652-8-1
ISBN 10: 0-9766652-8-X

Cover and Design by JJ Sargent

Library of Congress Control Number: 2005939154

This book is printed on acid-free paper.

Acknowledgments

My thanks and acknowledgments to the following journals, which have published or recently accepted the poems listed with them:

American Poetry Monthly: "Trackings"
Apostrophe: "Ankle-Deep in the Wallowa River"
Art Centering: "Metamorphosis"
Atlanta Review: "Seascape with the Fallen Icarus"
Bellowing Ark: "Weight-Bearing Effigies"
Birmingham Poetry Review: "Birds Asleep," "In the Straw-Bed,"
        "Somewhere Off the Freeways"
Carriage House Review: "His Name a Dying Legend," "The Revenant"
The Chaffin Journal: "For the Inglorious Dead"
The Chariton Review: "Villages"
Clark Street Review: "Ancestors"
Delmar: "Dolphins Near Volcanoes National Park," "The Visitation,"
        "Almost a Neighbor"
Descant: "Winter Wheat"
Ellipsis: "The First Coming"
The Gandydancer: "From Their Once-Secret Files"
Georgia Poetry Review: "The Bells of Amherst"
The Higginsville Reader: "Above the Id"
Hiram Poetry Review: "Ballad of Ponce de Leon in Florida"
The Hurricane Review: "The War Photographers"
Iodine Poetry Journal: "In Another Ithaca"
The Journal: "Breaking and Entering"
Kansas Quarterly: "The Future Miss America, Miss Troy"
The Ledge: "And What Rough Beast . . ."
Modern Poems of Ohio (anthology): "The Amish Farmer's Daughter"
North American Review: "Slices of Life"
Passages North: "*Der Rosenkavalier*"
North Dakota Review: "Drought"
Poem: "The Memoir"
Red Owl: "The Elegy Season," "Resurrection"
Samisdat: "Charisma"
The Small Pond: "Naming"
Stray Dog: "The Last Days of Sherlock"
Tar River Poetry: "Don Johnny," "'Sunday Afternoon on Grande Jatte
        Island'"
Wavelength: "From Dover Beach."

"The Amish Farmer's Daughter" appeared previously in *I Have My Own Song For It: Modern Poems of Ohio*. Edited by Elton Glaser and William Greenway (Akron: University of Akron Press, 2002)

Contents

Along a Well-Used Path
—for Paul L. Bennett, 1921-2002

Until his pain was too great, near the end,
he refused to take his cancer lying down
during its eight-year presence and slow spread
through his lower body. Gardener, poet,
mentor, long-time friend, he kept up
with his former students, daily walks
along the local bike path, and descriptions
of encounters there:

In the cool, leaf-dappled quiet
of October, near a bend at morning,
his dog tensed, quivering.
The undergrowth to their left parted.
A twelve-point buck stepped out, stopped on the asphalt,
turned and raised its antlered head
to front them in full, sinewed dignity.
Man and dog stood hushed with standing deer
in mutual respect, until the one
stepped away, off to the right, unhurried.

Gardener, poet, mentor, long-time friend,
gamely he made his way around the bend.

On a later day, the sun lay
low in the west. He squinted at the figure
gradually enlarging, treading its long shadow.
As it neared, his dog whined,
neck-hairs stiff. The man—it was a man,
though not like other cyclists, skateboarders
or walkers—paused to greet him
with a cold familiarity that he accepted
as his due, continuing
step by slow step toward the low-lying sun.

Gardener, poet, mentor, long-time friend—
WRITE ON! he told us. Right on, Paul,
right to the very end.

Part I

Dolphins Near Volcano National Park

Such swirls, such spoutings from the underworld
of water–from its depths more than two dozen
dorsal fins and sleek gray backs cavorting,
rising, plunging, circling in great arcs,
riding the surf like merry-go-round horses.
We've trudged across black lava beds
to reach the coast, out of temper
with the hot sun and foam-ruffled waves
until we see them. Sportive, sociable,
they seem possessed of something more
than instinct, in their fluent medium
conversing, high-pitched, as they frolic,
as if to tell us something.
But even if we had the instruments
to catch their beeps and chirpings, how could we
land creatures understand
such language? What is there to do
but sit in silence on dry rock,
viewing the syntax of their acrobatics,
aliens to their ocean-born esprit?

Birds Asleep

Rocked on the cradle of the deep,
great auks, kittiwakes and razorbills,
heads tucked under wet-proof wings,
bob to the Atlantic's troughs and swells.

White-tailed ptarmigans in full flight
dive into softly drifted snow
and sleep, like willow tits in Irmkutsk,
under blankets of protective cold.

Partridges and bobwhites form a ring,
heads facing outward, bodies pressed
for warmth together, seemingly alert
to danger as they rest.

Downward at dusk, from a Guatemalan
cane field the melodious blackbird
sounds its soothing whistle . . . lower, softer,
more widely spaced until no longer heard.

Some birds chortle in their slumber.
What does the common potoo sense
with eyes widening and shuttering
in its deep somnolence?

What do they dream, if anything,
those birds that twitch or flutter all night
as their warm blood, slowed by sleep,
funnels toward brain cells synchronized for flight?

How Darwin Would have Described It?

What hook-faced Caesar roosts in profile
before the plunge and pounce of its next kill?
The hawk perched on a tall, dead trunk
might serve as symbol for imperial

authority the Romans held in awe.
Though not plumed in beribboned khaki,
it's arrogant as any general
who's saved his nation from democracy.

Under its beak, a white, puff-feathered breast
swells like the stuffed shirt of a CEO,
its gray-flecked wings as neatly folded
as lapels. Below its coattails, though,

no shoes of soft Italian leather,
no spit-shined combat boots assert its status.
The image fails. The hawk waits there
with what evolved to serve it in the clutch:

its talons, clamped upon the tallest
wind-buffed, stricken tree within its scope,
its magisterial pose broken
with a hoarse shriek as it swoops,

wings, claws, beak extended.
It's only human to think of the field
mouse as a victim, to ascribe our lusts
and terrors to a raptor and its yield.

Why should a hawk be charged with such emotions
when it's merely fixed on its next meal?

Naming

After the sunset cooled and the sky dropped
dark reflections on the pond, I led
my son through shadows on the slow trail
back to our car. Moss and leaf-mold choked
our footfalls; a moon flickered the tall trees.
Neither of us spoke.

"The wind," I said—a stirring, a loud
sweep through the shivered boughs above us
down to silence where my son
stared at the turning leaves, flung
pale and then back to stippled olive green.
"Locusts," I said—"a grove of locust trees."

And later, "Crows," a hoarseness
clawing the night wind, thinning far
above us with the last upsweeping
shreds of storm. We reached the car;

my son hung silent at its door, turning
wide eyes upward, turning the tall trees
and cloud-sped moon, then grinned.
"Crows," he repeated. "Locust trees." "The wind."

Ankle-Deep in the Wallowa River

The quick twitch, corrugated tug
and surge of silver now squirms
coldly in my hand. *Too small*,
I judge, a strand of worm

strung from its mouth, the hook's point
lodged in the gristle of its throat.
With no bloodless way to coax
the barbed steel free, I twist it out

then ease my grip from red-frothed gills
returned to water. No life
flutters through them as the trout
floats belly sideways, bulged eye

staring at me as I stand
chill in the stream, fish-scales on my hand.

Trackings

How many hours separate from us
and from each other through the snow
of all last night they traveled
we cannot tell. On the sun-glazed
achingly bright field behind our farmhouse
tracks converge and criss-cross, one vast scroll
of hoofed, star-splayed, paw-etched itineraries.

A single deer had punched its double-toed
impressions through a sloping pasture's crust,
leading us down into the woods
where suddenly we come across fresh boot-prints
not ours, not those of a friend or neighbor,
leaping a fence, weaving through
a log-strewn, brambled neck of tree-growth
downhill, never breaking
into the open.
                    By the creek
another pair of boot-marks, parallel
but eight yards from the first, emerges,
plunges across our wagon–path to reach
another stretch of woods.
                    Apart, akin,
like railroad tracks receding,
the two sets crunch through shadow-fretted snow
and disappear beyond our fence-line
leaving us uncertain in the cold.

The Visitation

Once more the black dog's tearing
through our panicked sheep, his barking
frenzied, hurled beyond the lower barn.
The fields are crusted white, the moonlight
casts pale bluish shadows, yet once more
I reach for boots, down jacket, furry hat
and rifle, then crunch through the snow
to track his carnage and gain
one more shot at him.
                      The night is clear,
glazed, breathless, but it's hard to fix
precisely where he's raging.
Like fleecy thoughts the sheep have scattered—
a black form lunges at three
stragglers taking to the woods;
moments later something snarls among
a small herd on the open snow-slope,
too embroiled with legs, flanks, throats for me
to sight him cleanly.
                      When I fire
into the night sky, he knows my report,
halts his black fury, turns, and lopes off
through the woods, no fresh blood staining
his escape-tracks as it did once
when my aim was almost sure.
                      What's left
are limping, frightened sheep, not all
returning for my count—two lambs are lost.

Months later, with his blood-lust
only a faint memory,
I come upon a narrow white skull
bleached clean, globed, symmetrical
in the lush undergrowth of mid-July,
relic of the black dog's onslaught
recognized in near-tranquility.

And What Rough Beast...

I saw it from the farmhouse kitchen window.
No lamb of God. A lone sheep
standing mute, almost motionless,
half its face torn off.

No shepherds had watched over it by night.
When I went forth that cold December
to look upon its narrow skull-bone
bared under bloodied shreds of skin,

no manger offered room for it to lie.
There in the chill it stood, barely twitching,
one eye torn and hanging from a socket,
dumbly uncomplaining.

There must have been some sense to it,
some pain or numbed residual terror,
some brute response of prey to predator.
We stood in snow, the still waters frozen,

the once-green pastures crusted stiff and brown.
I could not kill it out of mercy,
wondering what held that eye-orb
glazed with infinite gray vacancy.

In the Straw-Bed

"If Dad was here…" He bites his lip
and scowls, his arm still dripping slime and blood.
She shakes her head without replying,
failed midwife with her fifteen-year-old son,
failed accoucheur.
                                    Old number 59,
tied to the stall, all bone-cage, hide,
and unborn calf, lies heaving. Each of them,
arm thrust almost shoulder-deep,
has tried to turn the oversized fetus
front legs down with head between.

As last resort, he hooks a winch
to block and tackle, pulls one massive foreleg
out of the womb, but nothing more
after each grating crank and strain.

"Stop," she says in a low voice. "Stop—
you'll only crack her pelvis. You can't save
your calf." "If Dad was here," he says,
unwilling to give up the unborn life
they'd promised him, unable to confront
whatever lay behind her stare.

His gaze drops to her waist, her flaring hips,
her crotch-tight jeans. "Your father wouldn't know…
There's only one way left to save her. Get the hacksaw."
"Why?" "You'll cut the foreleg off
and turn that calf *right*." "No. No, I won't."
He feels like sobbing. The cow groans
in useless labor. "All right, then.
I'll do it. Get the saw. You heard me—go!"

Black Angus near Dusk

Blended with the woods' deep shade
during the day's heat, they emerge now
shrugging their accustomed way
up a sloping pasture. In their full
luminous embodiment of being
what they are, they lend
a stolid dignity to the air around them
in the twilight, cows of vintage cowhood.
Bowing to their low-slung bellies' hunger,
they munch through clover-studded green,
slow-moving, unperturbed
as calves butt at their bulbous udders,
coal-dark faces smeared with milk.
Feeding their offspring or themselves,
they are the Peaceful Kingdom's chromosomes
made flesh, the fifth-day seed of Eden
grown to graze this evening's leaves of grass.

Drought

Our neighbor squints, glowering at the sun
glowing at him through a thick sky.
Furrows harden in his forehead,
in his fields the corn shrouds its stalks
with dry tatters. His sheep forage

our trampled creek bed, seeking shade
among the brown-crisped leaves falling.
His voice rasps at the children,
who've long gone without bathing. Water pumped
from both our springs oozes pale clay.

His wife no longer comes to visit
across the charred crunch of our front lawns.
We can hear heated words rising
from their kitchen, then his pick-up
revving off through dust-swirls.

Day after day his calves bawl,
tearing for milk at their mothers.
He curses, kicking brittle grass-clumps,
rousing a dark-winged whir of grasshoppers.
"Wish we could bring down rain," he says—

pacing our fence line with his Remington,
he scans the thick, glaring sky.
I nod, and can't think what to add
except a vision of his wife and kids
at gunpoint. "Dance!" he's yelling at them. "Dance!"

Winter Wheat

Too late to join the harvest—dawn
has long erased the constellated stars;
a combine has shorn half the field
to straw and stubble when I gaze upon

earth's buried, resurrected life,
its outcropped green of spring baked golden-brown
by mid-July, its bristled seed-heads
bowing to the sacrificial knife

machine-drawn now. Too late, too late
to view these bladed ears as sprouting from
the breasts of buried Indians
who, like Osiris, now regenerate

themselves as foodstuff. "Take and eat,"
Christ ordered his disciples, breaking bread,
transformed to flesh, with them. Too late
to cut my own swath through the ripened wheat,

I watch more tawny stalk-heads nod
into the mowing, threshing combine, then
flow from its chutes as virgin seed,
not yet the body of a son of God.

Breaking and Entering

No one could have really lived here—
a nine-by-twelve, box-like former pigpen
propped on boulders near our upper barn,
the wind tearing at its flaps of tin.
What girl could have spent her nights there?

No bed, no mirror—just this small,
dusty space pried open to the sunlight,
yielding its scant decor.
Hammer on hip, I clench a crowbar,
poking at the bald, armless doll,

the remnant cheesecloth drapery, the shreds
of wallpaper with floral print,
and then the shafted heart in red
lipstick, I LOVE DAVID on the wall.
Perhaps she lay here waiting for him, squeezed

behind the snarls of wire and scrap lumber
blocking its single-hinged door.
Perhaps this was her one poor privacy,
no room in the farmhouse for her,
or this had been her jerry-built playhouse

before the pigs dragged in to litter.
Who knows how long it had stood
before I took my crowbar to it?

Under its tin, the tongue-and grooved
roof-planks pull away like soggy cardboard,
the ceiling plaster yields to my shove
and I break through to find its hidden
lipstick heart, its full red words of love.

His Name a Dying Legend

A gray squirrel, startled, scurries up
the almost-bare branch of a maple,
like generations of its kind aware
of changing seasons and declining light,
of energy stashed in an acorn,
and now in an autumnal roar
as a bright orange middleweight Kubota
drags a Brouwer-VAC leaf suction,
Conestoga wagon-sized, across
our tree-strewn quad.
                              No present squirrel recalls
the thin-faced man with watery blue eyes
and dewlap neck, pausing
to lean a mottled cheek on rake-handle.
He's gone, except for a few reminiscent
flickers when we crunch through the flame
and pumpkin-colored leaves he swept each fall.

A tractor-hauled leaf suction would have eased
his labor, powered through piled maple-sheddings,
burning the distillate of long-dead trees.
We wouldn't then have dubbed him
Leif Raker, seen
as regularly as the gray squirrels
sweeping maple branches with their paws.
Maybe he knew what fossil fuel
he saved with arms and shoulders, felt fatigue
within the vast and part-recycled
entropy of seasons as he stood
within the swirl of ever-burning leaves.

Maybe he simply wore himself out
like his baggy overalls, a man
spending his body's store of energy,
replaced by Brouwer-VAC and bright Kubota,
a dying local legend.

The Elegy Season

Short days, long nights, the ground not frozen yet,
water still open in its small streams,
pooled for reflection:
                    Oh Narcissus,
this is the season when the flower
of your vain youth withers,
when maple leaves blaze toward extinction
or, brown and fallen, scurry to perform
a *Totentanz*, blown by the wind,
prelude to winter.
                    In their shaggy coats
Black Angus exhale ghost-white breath while grazing
the family graveyard on our neighbors' farm,
nudging fallen stones, the names and years
of those long underground
warmed by their moist nostrils as they munch
and ruminate the richly nourished green.

Frost shrouds our village cemetery
in glittering white; fall is well upon us,
vivifying old memorials.
In smoke from burning leaves the bittersweet
tang of mortality makes our eyes water.

Oh Orpheus, that backward look
that lost Eurydice—was it both cause
and symptom of nostalgia?

Our grounds have not yet frozen.
No grass looks greener than a pasture
under chill, bright sunlight in October
when deer lie dead along the road.

The Amish Father's Daughter
—for Bill Nichols

It's winter, and it's dark
with no electric lighting. I can't really
see her, but I'm told
that she has left the farmhouse
and has taken an old pair of skates
down to the pond.
                        The only light
is what the ice has just absorbed,
glinting it back toward pinpoint stars.
She should be warmly bonneted,
a long, dark woolen skirt around her calves,
not knowing, as she straps her skates on,
the figure she might cut against the snow—

a distant ancestress in Rheinland-Pfalz
who trudged across subzero farmland,
bent into the cold to steal some pleasure,
skimming on wooden blades her home state's
broadest river where it seemed
frozen over at its slow shallows.

Here in midwinter-chilled Ohio
it's probably as dark as on the Rhine
centuries ago. I've never seen her
mittened hands clasped behind her back
as she bisects the pond's perimeter,
serene and stately, smooth, each measured stroke
conserving as much virgin energy
as the surface freeze allows. Now she is
racing, soaring, whirling, sometimes
falling on her well-fleshed *popo*,
squealing, shrieking with laughter, letting it
all out, until she flops down
panting on a snow bank and dumps
ice shards from her boots.

How old is she? No one has said,
and it's too dark to tell. I know she's skating—
at home on an Amish farmer's spread of ice
sufficient to sustain her weight,
large enough to exercise her skills.

Villages

"Only the names of places had dignity."
—Ernest Hemingway, *A Farewell to Arms*

If only we still knew them . . .
If only our great grandparents
had spelled them for us . . . or our recent kin
driven from them down the long road
jammed with refugees.

If only we had listened . . .
folktales, family lore in which the word
for village twisted under tongue-tip,
not yet smoothed out like our names
at Ellis Island.

Not that we want the life itself
of villagers—the regimen of furrows
yielding potatoes, cabbage soup, a few
pigs to be killed for feast days.
Not that we want the maps of Central Europe

drawn back to the boundaries determined
by wigged heads, the state of villages
unchanged, the fiefdoms of great landholders
not yet leveled. What we crave
are places where our names reenter

local habitats—their trades, their long-known
feuds and marriages, if only
to assume the dignity
of weathered oaks and church towers, of gravestone
letters washing back into the soil.

Part II

Somewhere Off the Freeways

at Black Hand Gorge, or by some
gravel junction, we can still hear
trains dispersing their long loon-voweled
wail into the distance, mostly
in late afternoon, at suppertime
when few are near to witness.

We hadn't known those tracks rusting
out of sight in ever-narrowing
steel parallels still carried something.
We have no labor camps, have we,
no final destinations for our poor?

Perhaps these trains bear
only a few old tramps left over
from the Great Depression
or in their sealed boxcars hoard
long-exiled names that jounce and echo
out of nail-gouged lettering:
Nathan, Naomi, Jacob, Ruth.

But there's no profit in such baggage.
More likely they bring stone and brick
for the new Gatesian architecture
lording hillside farmland
gone to foreclosure, ironweed, and sumac.

Through Chickenville, past rural
trailer camps and the no-longer mobile
homes immured in cinder block
their metric click of wheels accelerates
a litany: *correct, correct, correct.*

Almost a Neighbor

Barely legible, his name
still marks one of the clustered
country mailboxes. Across the road
his box-like, metal-sided house stands
far back on a wind-blown slope
as he described it five months earlier.

He went by *Joe*—a gentle, quiet man
among us manic loudmouths.
Retired from the air force, wife dead,
children grown and distant, he'd fought
months of depression before entering
our fellowship of shared disturbances.

He told of helicopter piloting—
Korea first, then Vietnam.
Remembering how he'd been shot down
into jungle, I could understand
his choice to live on that bare, windy slope
I finally visited.

"We're almost neighbors," he said
when I told him of our farm;
but I was no good neighbor, couldn't bear
to check the loneliness up on that hillside
when I drove past. Except his name
gracing a tin box, barely legible,

I find no trace of him—house
locked shut and empty, no one living near
to ask about his absence.
Opposite a weed-choked driveway
his mailbox holds a few long envelopes
without a forwarding address.

Baptism: Dillon Dam

A hush descends upon the sand-smudged children;
bathers link arms at the beach's edge,
a scene arising from my childhood—
a human chain in waist-deep water,
a man immersing them, white clad.

my wife asks.

"A youngster, probably. That's how it was…
one by one held under, children
bathed in waters of eternal life,
elders singing."
             Here, the lifeguard's
striding yellow-shirted down the sand,
lifted megaphone a magnet
drawing one more chain into the water,
drawing me from memory.

Already the two chains of bathers,
arms linked, move toward one another
in a dance devoted to salvation,
deep ends bobbing, heads high, toes
touching lake-floor, wavering
then joining, waiting for their next command.

How slow their turning, both lines cleaving
rippled surface toward their starting points!
Should we join them? Sitting dry
and spellbound I can't tell.

Who's being saved? my wife asks again.
We turn to see a man in white
leaving an ambulance,
rushing toward the lifeguard's stand.
The chains are broken, bathers crowd around him.
No child has risen from the water
dripping, cleansed of sin.

Metamorphosis

At first they study the lake's stone
surface gleam, ignoring others
at the rim of the waves' splashed light
absorbed in slate-smooth deepening,

then nod to one another, bending
to unstrap, unbutton, wriggle
and emerge pale and glistening
above their two mounds of clothing

on the boulders where, but for the fur
patched on one chest and below
both bellies, they stand perfectly exposed.
Their eyes glaze.

Wearing the look of statues
or forgotten selves, they step through
the rippled slate-sheen as if numb
to all impressions, all consciousness

of people left on shore,
thrusting their bodies out and out
into the cold mountain water,
heads adrift among the surface stones.

Resurrection

Their skull-growths show first. Bulbous, bald,
like onions from their mounded earth
they burst through grave-plots, shedding palls,
shaking off dirt-crumbs, rubbing birth

into their mournful, cave-like eyes.
They will not stay where they belong;
leaving no stone unturned, they rise
shouldering aside the throngs

erupted headlong just before,
gaping and stretching, squinting down
at the next crop of upstarts—scores,
hundreds, thousands. Every town

adds to the groundswell. Mothers, sires
accost us, with their bony grasps
impede our progress. They require
food and concern, won't let the past

stay where we want it. With our lives
already squeezed and jostled, why
must we indulge them, or contrive
to shun their sad, reproachful eyes?

Between Illusions: Nullarbor

The two stand isolate, seeing clear
into a dead, level prospect,
sky a clamped-down bowl of heat,

the rails'clack-clack ebbing,
the Indian Pacific
a mere glint receding

straight as a ruler's edge, bisecting
vacant land where it disgorged them,
pale red crossroads

traced over sun-bleached stretches of their vision;
nothing to raise even the shimmer
of mirage—Australia's *Nullarbor*,

crude Latin, "no trees"—
nothing that grows above their thighs,
nothing but the distance-tapered criss-cross

of steel tracks and sleepers,
nothing of oceanic waters
from thirty million years ago,

nothing but absence magnified
of which they form a miniscule
twin nucleus; nothing but two humans

unprotected from flies gathered
under the insistent sun,
waiting for a four-wheel drive

to transport them to a mission
for the Aborigines
more than a hundred miles off in the outback.

Chena Hot Springs

In winter, the aurora borealis
paint the sky like a mad northern
Van Gogh—arches, streamers,
swirlings, bursts of color
in the endless night sky.

Here in June, the sky hangs
dripping, a gray sponge
punctured by tall spruce and pine.
Rain dribbles down the lodge's
picture windows. Moose

graze the roadside nearby.
Up from Fairbanks, a few families
steam in the hot baths
where miners once paid gold
to soak the ache from their backs.

Most rental cabins now yawn empty.
"You should be here when the Lights perform,"
a Scotch drinker tells us in the lodge.
"You couldn't buy yourself a room here, though.
We're booked solid for the next two winters."

He shows us the resort's menu,
printed in two languages. "Plenty
high-tech Japanese. Young newlyweds
who want their firstborn to be male,
who believe that... under Northern Lights..."

He lets us consummate the image—
two bodies intertangled, straining,
panting to become one
with the cosmos in an energy-burst
seeding a son if favored by the skies.

The Bells of Amherst

1879: Dear Cousins,—
Did you know we had a fire here,
and that for the whim of the wind
Austin and Vinnie and Emily would have been homeless?
We were waked by the ticking of the bells—
the bells tick in Amherst for a fire,
to tell the firemen.

How many fires burned in old towns of once-
Puritan New England? Salem, too,
possessed its chronicler of flames—
those in a lime-kiln
gnawing at the bones of Ethan Brand,
or glowing in domestic hearths and hearts,
or in Earth's Conflagration.

The moon was shining high at the time,
the birds singing like trumpets.
Vinnie came soft as a moccasin,
"Don't be afraid, Emily,
it is only the fourth of July"

I could hear buildings falling,
and oil exploding, and people walking
and talking gayly, and cannon soft as velvet
from parishes that did not know
that we were burning up.

In Salem Hawthorne loved attending fires
that he deemed worth watching,
gazing at both flames and firemen
"to the great indignation" of some townsfolk.

And so much lighter than day it was,
that I saw a caterpillar
measure a leaf far down in the orchard.

It's said that Hawthorne sent his sister
into the night to judge the fires
and report to him if they were worth
his getting out of bed for.

1881: *We had another fire.*
Monday a week ago, at two in the night.
After a night of terror, we went to sleep
for a few moments, and I could not rise.

The fire bells are oftener now,
almost, than the church bells.
Thoreau would wonder
which did the most harm.

On Your Evening Constitutional

By moonlight you can't help seeing
the two men running, hear breath sputtering
from the heavyset one like air
from a loosely tied balloon,
the scarecrow figure gaining on him.

By Jove, it's not your fault the street
slants uphill for that fat bloke. Who knows?—
Maybe they're an ill-matched pair of joggers.
Maybe they've made a wager—last one
to the tavern buys the beer.

Something glints in the scarecrow's hand.
Of course it could be a peace offering
of silver coins, but you regret
not carrying the heirloom Lugar
lifted from a corpse in World War II.
Perhaps the heavyset man's innocent,

and scarecrow wants to kill him,
and if you stepped in you'd become
an accessory. More likely, they don't know
each other—merely running
separately, through moonlight, home to bed.

Of course they could be actors practicing
some confounded outdoor drama—
bloody nuisance, these theatre people
crowding into the neighborhood!
And don't you have the right to be too old

to huff and puff, catch up to them
and ask what in tarnation's going on?
You've had your bit of exercise—
that heavyset chap needs it more than you do.
And what about your evening glass of wine?

Terrorism at the Shopping Mall

I must avoid being conscious
of the arrogance displayed by showcase models,
their elegant synthetic bodies
robed in furs,

and mustn't risk a guess at the true cost
of the diamonds glittering in beds
of velvet-looking plush.

I shouldn't take to heart the small print
on tags betraying the origins
of gaudy silk shirts, denims, brand-name
gym shoes, racks of sale-priced jackets,

or ponder trademarks on imported
videos and cybernetic games,
lest I become prone to their violence

programmed for push-button entertainment,
and come to fear the terror
linked to underground world labor,

linked to the consuming guilt and rage
I'd feel ready to explode
if I couldn't let it all out
in a burst of spending.

Did Dante Know?

The truly damned are those in whom hell
fosters not mere graceless acquiescence,
but loyalty as well.

They boast that brimstone air attests
to productivity, and wear their favorite
brands of torture lettered on their chests.

Chamber of Commerce zealots glow at
endless public barbecues. Their welcome wagons
toot for the visiting Italian poet.

Oh how they love their rituals of boredom,
backbiting and self-abasement, taking pains
to justify the moral order.

And when they greet new converts, they grin
knowingly at me, as smug as sin.

The Future Miss America, Miss Troy

Beauty she took to be her birthright,
her ticket to adventure and escape,
its own excuse for being. With the swan
as sire and model, she kept faith

in beauty all through ugly ducklinghood,
scrubbing at freckles, drinking diet wine,
molding her angles into winsome curves.
The Spartan envoys noticed how refined

her gestures seemed. She practiced smiling, took
ballet and drama, learned to cheer for male
athletics and, because she so loved Paris,
to trust in Trojans. When the Greeks set sail

she gave her name to pulchritude—the goal
of strategists and queen of pin-up girls.
Her brow still gleams with tinsel crown or laurel,
her swan's nape graced by hyacinthine curls.

Waving from float or chariot,
past rusted scrap, the battered walls of Troy,
the ghost-town GM factories of Flint
and armies of the maimed or unemployed,

she holds herself a citadel of smiles,
gazing sweetly on disaster, pleased
to service such a fallen world with beauty,
her one known truth, self-certain, value-free.

Seascape with the Fallen Icarus

Along a North Sea marshland, black shapes
settled in the distant shallows
look like sea-birds swarmed down
from a great migration. Reeds, marsh-grass

glisten nearby as the tide seeps
inland, dark, glinting a few
sharded rainbows where the low sun
burns through haze. Offshore

the hull of a huge tanker rises
calm on the ink-black wash, the sky
dissolving into water, the slow lap
of tide-swell bearing clumps of seaweed

and Icarus washed up among the reeds,
his charred wings slick with crude oil.
Larger than any sea-bird, he
compels attention to the scene's

right foreground, where his corpse intrudes
its tainted mythic presence into
what could be a modern masterpiece
in oil on brackish water.

Part III

The War Photographers

"Hold still!" the war photographers
commanded, and the dead obeyed.
Like vultures, they sought carrion.
Hunched beneath their black-fledged shades

near horse-drawn darkrooms, needing long
exposure for their corpse-filled plates,
the young disciples of Daguerre
stayed out of battle, forced to wait

for clearing air and subjects prone
to unheroic poses. Drained
of brilliance, graven by the sun,
their photos ghosted each campaign—

Bull Run, Antietam, Gettysburg—
each still-death showing twisted gray
faces gaping at their crude
optic technology. Had they

lived later, when with laser-beamed
precision death could be devised,
would they have trusted what was once
their realm of slits and naked eyes?

From Dover Beach

- 6 June 1944

Land's end and water, early dawn,
bow, stern, and port emerge as blurs
at the horizon—who can tell
what fate awaits their passengers?

Arnold's sea of faith has ebbed,
Lord Tennyson would cross the bar;
his restless, aged Ulysses vowed
to pry the Western Gates ajar.

In lieu of Christian afterlife,
with grey hulls aiming off from shore,
they held the fear of death at bay
with oceanic metaphor.

Brave men, these stock Victorians
who, captains of the soul, embarked
toward a huge void—or were they merely
bo'suns whistling in the dark?

The dark gives way to gray light. Ships
line offshore waters, landing craft
dangled from larboard. Men in khaki
gather fore and aft,

helmets removed, to kneel in prayer.
What can their chaplains say, to shrive them?
"Oh Lord of hosts, of thunderheads
and high explosives, of the drive

to mate and murder, who impels
our love of life and mortal dread,
give courage, that these men may chance
the odds against them lying ahead."

The sea ebbs. Lowered landing craft
draw heavy fire from the beach.
Disgorged on groin-deep sandbars, troops
wade deathward with no saving turns of speech.

Marching Toward Mesopotamia

Let us go then, you and I,
where the desert stretches toward a sky
dusky as a shroud of desolation.
Let us go, past torched oil wells,
mangled convoy trucks and mortar shells
along the track of armored vehicles
past Ur and Uruk, Kufa, Babylon,
site of the world's first skyscraper fallen
to Ground Zero, then restored
as Nebuchadnezzar's palace—past the hoarded
statues in Sumerian grave plots
and a four thousand year-old ziggurat.

From their height the bombers hit or miss
findings of archaeologists.

Or if we journey south with well-armed Kurds,
we might pay homage to the disinterred
bronze figurines of Nineveh. There might
be time, there might be time, to view the site
of bas-reliefs at Nimrud, age-old clay,
before their palace walls give way
to the advances of a modern army.

The Assyrian came down like the wolf on the fold
And his cohorts were gleaming in purple and gold.
The wolf, turned fox in a guerilla war,
nips at the flanks of our Elite Corps.

I am no Alexander, my good friends.
Am an attendant voice for CNN.
I have seen the medics' battlefield *triage*
and masked my mortal dread in camouflage.
Before Samara's spiral minaret
becomes a dust-heap, I may yet
reach Baghdad, where the mosque of Kadhimain
might hold its intricate tile patterns from the reign
of air-strikes, and where muezzins once could bare
frail flesh toward heaven in their calls to prayer.

I do not think that they would pray for me.

Der Rosenkavalier
—May 15, 1945

Munich in ruins, rubbled Nuremberg
unready for its trials later that year—
I found him in his Garmisch villa,
composer of *Der Rosenkavalier*,

*Ein Heldenleben, Salome, Also
Sprach Zarathustra*, and the other scores
I knew and loved. Erect and rosy-faced
at eighty-one, he greeted me outdoors,

his first "Yank" visitor-reporter since
war's end. I glanced around his trim estate.
Hadn't the past few years affected him?
"Ja, ja, they tried to relocate

some bombed-out people with me. In my house."
His neck-veins swelled, his voice rose. "Strangers! Here!"
His finger trembled, pointing through a blossomed
garden at his villa. "Papa dear,

calm down. It never happened, *Gott sei Dank*,"
his slight, non-Aryan-looking son's wife said.
"It would have if the war had gone on, though.
It seems *der Fuehrer* never even read

my protests and appeals." I asked what else
he held against Herrn Hitler. "His poor taste.
Forever Wagner. He and others, while
my own last opera was never staged.

And then my problems with *The Silent Woman*—
Stefan Zweig composed its words for me.
A clever text, and how was I to know
of race-laws back in 1933?"

Had he considered leaving Germany
when such conditions limited his art?
He arched his eyebrows. "What? And leave my source
of income? Leave the country of my heart?"

His fine south-German tenor rang out. "Here
are eighty opera houses, maybe more."
"Here *were* your opera houses," I corrected.
He seemed not to have heard, or to ignore

my interruption. *"At least eighty!"*
Then, gesturing toward Alice, his son's wife—
"Allow me to assert that she remained
the only Jewess free in the Third Reich."

"Free? *Nein*, Papa, it was more like house arrest.
I couldn't hunt. I couldn't even ride."
"Hush, darling. My good sir, our interview
perhaps should end soon. Pardon the false pride

of someone of the old school if I offer—"
he gave a dry, self-deprecating laugh—
"in honor of your visit, a true copy
of my professional, signed photograph."

A halting, haunting, slightly dissonant
nostalgic waltz—*der Rosenkavalier*—
lilted my memory. I stared at him,
then shook my head. His thin smile disappeared,

he bowed, and as we said *auf Wiedersehen*
I sensed him, with his lip curled, judging me—
Another crude American. Too crass
for music, culture, sensibility.

For the Inglorious Dead

Antinoos, Eurymachus, Peisandros—
by dying earned the immortality
of Homer's verse. Able,
Baker, Charlie—killed
at Kasserine Pass when they turned and fled
a German tank attack. Euryades,
Eurydamos, Leokritos, Polybus—
suitors galore feasted on the herds
of Ithaca, and tasted death
upon Odysseus's homecoming.
Dogface, Franklin, Garfield—sodden corpses
washed ashore on some Pacific atoll,
rifles gone, boots filled with sand.
Agelaos, Elatos, Melanthios—
too many to recount here. Like caught fish
twitching away their choked lives on the beach,
so lay the suitors heaped on one another.
Heinrich, Ludwig, Wolfgang—bodies frozen,
face down, in the snow near Stalingrad.
Think of the bronze and stone memorials
all over Europe and America
after two world wars. Lest we forget:
slaughter is indiscriminate. Whether facing
Odysseus's wrath and fighting back
or pleading for mercy, swarming
with desperate gusto over the top
or forced at bayonet point from their trenches,
the brave and cowardly fall side by side,
listed vertically by alphabet
or lined by a blind bard. The dead don't care,
and Homer never claims that life is fair.
Whoever thinks that life or death should be so
might just as well beseech a raging bull
"Halt, noble beast. Do not impale me.
I'm a vegetarian."

In Another Ithaca

O ruined sire, lost for twenty years
fighting for your so-called Fatherland
and holed up in a cavern where the Cyclops
held you POW—don't try
to reassert yourself.
                              You come home weak,
bewildered by the changes. Mother, too,
lost confidence in your return,
married the wisest of her suitors,
brought about reform. O father,
how it hurts to see you
showing your war wounds and your Iron Cross
to ancient serving maids and swineherds.
We have become a peaceful little kingdom.
Why should we honor you?

Why should you call to mind my early boyhood
with you looming tall, resplendent
in your officer's regalia, your troops
disciplined to die for the Third Reich?
I am a man now, father, self-sufficient,
re-educated, while you cling to life
in shame for having lost your whole battalion,
a pensioner-to-be, a burden for us,
Exhibit A of your famed shrewdness
in the tactics of survival.

Better to have fallen
near the battered walls of Troy
now being restored with aid
from those you once regarded as your allies.

Slices of Life

Was Homer blind in overlooking
the six other Troys stacked
like geo-literary strata?
Too many for a single epic
which would have burst its Greek hexameters
had it applied its inventories
to the masses in their mass graves
with their mounds of ancient bric-a-brac—
even Whitman's leaves would only gloss
the surface of those bone-heaps.

The epic version of antiquity
would suffer overcrowding if we tried
to multiply The *Iliad* by seven,
the rise and fall of cities through armed conquest
and all those vaunting heroes.
That shattered kitchenware, those amulets
to guarantee fertility, those rubbled
chunks of pre-Achaean urban housing
suggest another fate for the seven Troys,
buried under generations of their own
solid waste. Think of Homer
numbering such tons of household trash
or Whitman as a census-taker
touting the lists of garbagemen on strike.

The Memoir

An old man's verbal craft—
to hold the mirror up to his own past.
Reflections—painful, if he lets them be.
What sort of immortality,
self-edited ahead of time for those
remembering him through his prose,
should he expect? His two divorces, lust
for recognition, son's death, cowardice—
how can he squirm his way through all those years
if other old men, knowing his career,
survive, and their reviews of him persist?
Must he confess himself as his own priest?
Self-conscious image-maker, he well knows
the ravaged face his mirror shows
each morning when he shaves, the near-bald skull,
memento mori, unavoidable
model of what's to come. Alas,
poor Yorick, hoisted from the rich soil as
a stark, instructive symbol! With such fate
staring him in the eyes, is it too late
to make amends, interpret, justify
a life no worse than others authored by
his erstwhile friends? No Hamlet, he has no
Horatio willing to forego
felicity for him. An old man must
invest in his own memory and trust
in understanding readers—now, before
time tells, on him, a different story.

Underground

Often there's water down there, dark
as my eyeball, giving back
my own reflection where I shine a light.
Some cranium-shaped caves drip stalactites
while the water's seepage, in its slow
alkaline corrosion,
gnaws at their skulls.
                          The underground can rise
like resurrection into consciousness
or beckon a descent
into pre-history, a labyrinth
where Theseus confronted an old nightmare
out of myth, but where
cave-dweller art did better, taming
wild beasts into sketches of big game
on sheltered rock walls.
                          Comrades, go
underground if you would know
of death and origins or the half-life
of nuclear waste. Think of a dark river
flowing forever
under your dreams, stone steps leading down
to a stone pier, the black prow
of a skiff half-buried
in water as its boatman ferries
nameless shades across.
Or would you finger small gold necklace crosses,
groping for life eternal when, in Rome,
you wander through the catacombs,
an underground of bones and martyrdom
suffered for a Kingdom yet to come?

Dig down, dig down, to where a bronze-tooled axe
lies buried with a chieftain's artifacts.
Squeeze through an oozing birth canal of rock
and slither down and back
into the chamber where a little blind
life heaves its gills. You'll find it
in that dark pool where you flash your light,
deeper than reflection. Curl up tight
against the stone floor. Listen. There,

even farther underground, you'll hear
the river coursing
through an old vein. No one knows its source.

Ancestors

I.
Imagine them on straw pallets
laboring for heirs, succeeding, leaving
crosses in some parish register
or churchyard. At what distance do we bear
portions of their fractured chromosomes?

No family tree, no long-traced lineage,
only a smoke-dimmed image:
by firelight our greatest grandmothers,
deep-eyed peasants, squinting, stitching clothes
for their descendants, rousing to the needs
cried out from sleep. Which of them sleep
in our restless beds of flesh and bone?

II.
They dreamt in their own languages—
once-fertile fields, diasporas,
pre-natal infants strangled in the womb,
crying for life, for a second chance—
and woke determined to cut ties
to their motherlands, across wide water
seeking another dream, in a new language,
in tenements, decaying brownstones,
sweat-shop factories, by pushcart street-sales
dreaming for us, their children
or their children's children, freed
by birthright from their Old World accents.

III.
Try to remember or imagine—
they walked ahead in their own visions,
too quick for us, yet linked
by sweaty palms. When they paused
in front of shops to talk of war,
unemployment, politics,
time expanded on the sidewalk
until they felt our tug and smiled,
speaking our names to tall strangers,
proud to have us shake their hands.

They bundled us into the back seats
of old Fords and drove enormous miles
before we woke outside a small town
where we counted freight cars
clanking across the road. Hours later
they steered us into Cleveland or Detroit,
shaded streets, a house that smelled of ointment
where a Grandma hugged us, uttering
endearments in a half-choked foreign tongue.

They urged our schoolwork, scrubbed and combed us—
confirmation class, dance lessons,
first dates. Having known disaster,
they sat up heavy-eyed till we got home.
With friends, we grew embarrassed by their clothes;
their speech was thick, old-fashioned,
ignorant of styles and movie stars.

They lived to see us college-trained and married,
bearing their descendants in the suburbs
where we moved with our promotions.

They moved too, south—their lives, our history
ensconced in a pink condominium,
photos for a family album,
and a few lyric poems.

From Their Once Secret Files

My other self, part *me*, part fiction,
part other man of flesh and blood,
prowled through suspicions of the State Police,
behaving as their dossiers said he should.

More married to my wife than I am
because he bears the family name she's kept,
he's more likely to be European.
Our bureaucrat-biographers, adept

at reading between the lines of private mail,
found in my wife's letter to a friend
being trained for the consulate in East Berlin
two mentions of her husband, John. Transcending

my more limited existence, this *John Winter*,
my other self compiled from wiretaps,
filched mail and infiltrated records,
lived on under wraps,

more widely traveled
and more adventurous than home-grown *me*,
posing as a family man but serving
the U.S. Information Agency.

Perhaps I'll find him
haunting a World Book Fair in what was once
East Germany. He'll frown up from his text,
perplexed by my part-strangeness, part-resemblance.

Profiling

We are all foreigners here. Shadow persons.
Assume, sir, that at least provisionally
we exist, though not yet verified
by measured, discrete pieces of ourselves.

Perhaps, were you to read me
through the eyes of that Cambodian
also applying for residence, I'd be
as strange and threatening as any Other—

a sinister smile with no beard attached,
my nose hooked like a scimitar,
skin ambiguously colored.
Called up to your desk, I hear my name—

three untranslated words as void of meaning
for you as the passport-photo face
they momentarily connect with,
glossing over my distinctiveness—

Hair: brown. No encroaching gray?
Eyes: brown. One of those four colors
you're allowed, which means no bloodshot red.
You type each datum, answered to your queries,

onto a blue ID card, confident
that after dismantling
your state police could jigsaw-puzzle me
back to a fugitive, full-bodied self.

Above the Id

Ego can mask itself as friend—
right hand gripping, pumping, firm
backslap or bear-hug, bluff-voiced to defend
against potential enemy or worm

of self-doubt. Ego needs to take its bow
after each intricate, well-practiced dance.
Though art be long, it begs top rating now,
hero of its own romance.

Ego can swell to godhead at the crotch,
stoked with creative juices, can mistake
its words for revelation, though it watch
itself revert to babble, self-possessed.
Yet sometimes it curls in a straw-bed, naked,
howling for milky love from Mary's breast.

Don Johnny

No hell remains beyond the yawning
spectators who know me
too well at this stage:
a painted backdrop, one more
wooden female, one more conquest
hunched and jerky to the pulled strings.

Punchinello laughs. An organ
grinds out one more rote performance:
no soaring notes of Mozart
pitched against the cold Stone Guest
avenger, guilt and passion joining
urgent in my double-edged motif.

Where are the violins,
the orchestrated scores, the worthy
genres? No more fires
burn for the once-forbidden act;
no more drama builds upon each
newly swollen figure of my triumph.

Charisma

He smiled at the photographers
and at all public functions, smiled
at women in the corridors
and at his mirrored smile of self-approval
until he turned into his chosen image,
a purse of lips snapped open, oral charm
transfixed into a nation's symbol—
the Great American Mouth:

Envy of all undernourished peoples,
arch and gleaming gateway
into a country's heartland through its gut:
the mouth of school kids giving the Bronx cheer
to teacher's pets, crying in the kitchens
"Hey, Mom, I knocked 'em dead today!"—
the sugar-teat mouth, stuffed with sweets
for bellowing its needs and triumphs
louder than others, the mouth of Texas
oil-gushers, headline-screeching news-hawkers,
Irish lovers of the Blarney stone:

The mouth that swallows diet Coke and Lite Beer,
pops pills, crunches pale inflated corn,
smirks at Polack jokes and leers at coeds,
the mouth that's launched a thousand quips
and burnt the corkless tubes of nicotine,
an advertiser's opening and trap,
a mouth that sucks,
licks, breathes hard, salivates,
a mouth in search of a kindred orifice
to kiss or swirl its tongue in:

An organ piping up for Mouther's Day,
Mickey Mouth, the old pre-bellum Mouth
of Bible-quoting, Shakespeare-honeyed hams—
for all day-suckers, college cheers, free
enterprise and golden crowns of dentists,
rightward leading, yes indeeding
before it thinned out
                    under our very noses.

Part IV

In the Widowed Professor's House
—for Wallace Irwin, Jr.

He still mourns the emptiness she left:
one side of their heirloom bed,
her place beside his in the breakfast nook,
her disembodied perfume
lingering in drawers and closets.

The house remains for him to manage.
Grief can be swept from a remodeled kitchen.
The bathroom has become a plumber's dream
of creature comforts, foolproof fixtures
gleaming with reassurance
for unstable widowers, the living room
a study in snug order where he settles
into being most himself—collected
in his thoughts, in his one easy chair
at peace with a cantankerous old body
and the ache of lost commitments.

The room is still. No television.
No console set to occupy
excessive space or time. A desk lamp
bends its gooseneck toward a surface cleared
for his distinctive penmanship.
A wicker-backed chair still upholds
the rigor of his scholarly research.
Behind the desk, his massive bookcase
covers an entire wall:

detective novels, literary journals,
multi-volume works of Goethe,
Schiller, Edward Bulwer-Lytton,
age-old classics lengthening their shelf lives,
tax forms, alphabetically filed lectures,
notes from the audited course of a lifetime,
and in the largest pigeonhole
a glass of grape juice for his medications.

Outside, the slur of traffic on his street
has thinned to an infrequent murmur.
His study window has long ceased

its import of the evening light,
reflecting now the room's illumination.
He leafs through a book,
trying to slow his reading, trying
to focus on a passage into sleep.
Oh Mary! he remembers her warm breath
against his neck, her living stay against
the old encroachment of insomnia.

The night grows heavy with his sorrow.

Short-Term Employment

For the last few years I've worked
at my vocation of senility.
Mile after mile I wander through the house,
thinking, "What did I want to do or look for?"
Having lost the art of least resistance,
I've taken up jogging through the alphabet,
hoping to run across the first letter
of a friend's name, then the stubbornly
elusive name itself. My tongue-tip sags
under the words I can't quite recollect.

Even the usual morning rituals—
tooth-brushing, shaving, breakfasting—require
extra devotion, or become neglected.

Somewhere in my attic, I assume,
stashed with souvenirs, diplomas,
photo albums, useless scraps of lumber,
there's a Certificate of Competence—
a recent one—if only I could find it;
and in the bedroom's near-dark
I'm startled half to death by a man
suddenly confronted in the mirror—
threatening, bewildered.

Loose Connections

The spindly steel-grid tower
blinks on-off
on-off,
its nerve-like impulses
signaling for cell phone voices.

Cells
that go dead,
swell or crowd out other cells.
On-off, on-off,
I'm at a loss
to explain such circuits,

overloaded or short circuits.
Tell me about their impulses,
ganglia, synapses.
Tell me while I still can hear you,
while you still have voice.

Tell me before the long-familiar
furniture in these rooms
and these rooms themselves darken,
before I'm at a loss to tell you
what we ate for dinner last night.

Look.
Look hard around us.
Faces we believed would never
leave us are already
lost to memory.
On-off, on-off

our local tower keeps pulsing
for clear cellular connections—
no stuttering, no flickering
I'm at a loss to deal with
before the loudest voices,
the largest headlines in the world

trail off to nothing .

The Last Days of Sherlock

He paces through his logic. Padded walls
close in on him, but can't restrain
his mind. The door's glass porthole,
sunk within its heavy, steel-rimmed frame,

blazes with clarity. He knows
when Dr. Watson peers beneath each door
for data, when the head nurse comes and goes
with coded heel-taps, when the corridor

lies empty—breathless, fraught
with clues for his true mission on the ward.
The keyhole's arch design betrays a plot
being hatched against him. Like a long-held chord

the interplay of every fact
throbs to his insight. Sniffing at his food,
mouthing his pills, he tries not to attract
attention to his shrewdness,

waiting for that one click
when his door swings open, spies discard
their useless guises, and the night-shift medic
proves to be a man from Scotland Yard.

Ballad of Ponce de Leon in Florida

The flatness of this land gives rise
to many a strange mirage beyond
the sun-struck condominiums
and fairways fringed by shimmering ponds;

and many another man in search
of lasting youth and energy
has been deceived. I should have known
that what I sought was not to be

discovered on this earth—a spring
for all our winters, rinsing blight
and torpor from our flesh, renewing
generative appetite—

not on this earth but in a mix
of *dep, teg, thol, zine, nil* or *zac,*
alchemic capsules, compounds veiled
in symbols of the zodiac.

Not from a fountain did I need
to quaff; the water in a mug
sufficed when it enabled me
to gulp a wonder-working drug.

I gulped. *Caramba*! I could feel
my armor lighten, a weight lift
from off my spirit. God be thanked—
a new man swelled my frame, as if

cleansed of the taint our father Adam
deeded us after Eden. Now
retired, carefree, member of
the local country club, endowed

with pills enough to last a lifetime,
I leave mirages to the poor,
my timeworn, creaking self disposed
to hang with my sword behind the door.

The Annunciation

Suppose it came to you,
not out of the proverbial blue
but dragging its wings up your front walk,
hook-nosed, like a wounded hawk.
Would you let it in, to kneel
before you and recite some spiel
about your being the Chosen One?
If so, you'd think someone had blundered—
such a decrepit specimen
of the Angelic Host to send
on such a mission! And to *you*?
Ye Gods! It looks like it's been through
the wars, and probably has. Not
a pleasant prospect. You had thought
that, being chosen, you could gain control
of psychic energy, of heart and soul
for those devout and humble folk below you,
like some Dalai Lama CEO,
not being shot at, starved, burnt at the stake,
or hammered crosswise, for Chrissake!
Just by seeing such a poor excuse
for a divine messenger, you'd lose
all trust in it and say,
Get lost, angel.
If I need inspiration, I'll immerse
myself in my own study, writing verse.

The Revenant

Where is the fountain where we shared
our few crumbs with the city's pigeons?
The plaza, as you see, is still here,
bordered by luxury shops catering
to Western tourists. After the Regime
tumbled, monuments and fountains
ranked as showpiece symbols of the State.
The water now feeds these four
beds of imported tulips.

Where is Emil's bookshop, where we swore
secrecy and laid plans for a just
and democratic future?
                    Emil died
soon after you were forced to flee the country.
The Party seized his shop and used it
for its own corrective fictions.
Then your democratic future
swept in. The shop changed hands.
If you've a taste for porno,
Japanese massage, or a quick fix,
pay the place a visit.

Why have you let this happen?
Old man, you've been in exile too long,
basking in your ideals.
We've had to stay and make a living.

Why are there beggars here? Is there no law
against these prostitutes? Where are the State Police?
You've got your laws confused. Remember—
this is democracy and the free market.
No State policeman dared to show his face
after we exposed them. You
should know what went on with those scoundrels.

Where are my comrades from those...
those times before the crackdown?
The city's parks retain much of their former
verdant charm, my friend. Their shaded benches
seat more than a dozen drowsy

old utopians. Perhaps
you'll recognize them—reminiscing,
still sharing crumbs with squirrels and pigeons.

All of us—we dreamt of something different.
Even in the West I kept on dreaming.
Dreams are confusions of an idle mind,
my friend—fulfillments of lost hopes.

I know, I know.
In dreams our dead comrades come alive
and speak to us, not as mere graven statues.
The past invades and occupies
the present—time-dissolving,
unhistorical.
                    And immaterial,
as Marx would say, old friend.
Wake up! Let physical reality—
your city, now—
seep back into your senses. Look around you—
not at the litter or graffiti,
but at the new cars, renovated buildings,
shoppers free to buy or not buy
what they choose. Aren't they what you dreamed?

But all these young people
with their head-sets, ear-phones,
faraway looks. They bump into me
as if I'm not here. Have I gotten lost?
Where have you been, old man?
It's not the revolution Marx predicted.
Haven't you heard of cybernetics
conquering space in record time,
available *now* to the masses,
their credit being the future tense of money?

Where is the fountain where we gathered,
where the water leapt in sunlight
high above its own polluted source—
above the stir and flow, the surging
at our city's heart?

The Tooth

—lost by Jana Cerna, daughter of "Kafka's Milena"

Until a second woman brought the tooth
Milena, suffering a gum disease,
had pulled from her own jaw in Ravensbrueck,
she could still feel
Mumsy wasn't really dead.
She was cold to the first
visitor-survivor, black-shawled,
standing at her Prague doorstep
distant from the concentration camps,
to tell her she'd been orphaned.

She was old enough, street-wise enough
no longer to believe in tooth-fairies,
in gifts left under the sweet-smelling
heart-shaped pillow Mumsy used to plump
when bidding her sweet dreams,

but young enough to view Mum's tooth as keepsake,
part of the mouth that once had talked to her,
a rotted chunk of that elusive smile
she'd seem too seldom, and could seldom fathom.
She couldn't live with, couldn't give it up,
that almost-living shard
of someone so irrevocably dead.

She put the tooth in a safe place
lost to memory, and wrote:
"I believe that human beings
have the inalienable right to forget—
that this is one of our few freedoms
no one can take away."

She was young then,
but old enough to know what it was like
to be the daughter of a famous woman—
mistress of artists, flaming journalist,
member of the Czech resistance movement.
She lost the tooth somewhere,
her mother lost already

to a grave near Ravensbrueck,
to party-line historians
who called her Trotskyite and thus annulled her,
to writers who would see her only
as Kafka's two-year prop and confidante.

Jana, though, was old enough
to know how it must feel
to pull one's own tooth without Novocaine
inside a concentration camp,
old enough to know of amputees
who still ached where the flesh had been,
though she had never lost a limb—
only her Milena.

But she was tough, her own resistance fighter,
street-wise, knowing what it was to lose
sobriety, blood, one-night stands,
and fairy-tale good Mumsies.
Too old to give full trust to pain-killers,
smuggled drugs or alcohol,
she tried to trust in her forgetting
where an aching tooth had been,
setting her jaw hard, so as not to cry out
"Mother! Mother!"

The Organ Grinder and the Monkey

Once upon a not-long time ago
in a not-too-foreign city,
an organ grinder plied what many
took to be his humble trade
with beggar's cup and barrel organ
on the busy streets of Prague.

To fill his cup and feed his belly,
the organ grinder bought a monkey,
a Chinese sage-faced, skull-capped mimic
who grinned and winked at normally staid burghers
on the gas-lit streets of Prague.

For his gathered onlookers
the organ grinder and his pet
belonged together, like Czech bread and jelly—
the humble man, the monkey like a child
outrivaling an older brother,
wooing Mom and Dad.
And when the organ grinder played his organ
the monkey sometimes played with his,
a cute pink thing that gave him pleasure
all the more when modest blushes
pinked the cheeks of peeking maidens.

But all was not well. Soon the monkey
started turning his red rear-end
against the organ grinder's will,
adding a fillip to their street performance.
Thus ensued a painful parting,
man from monkey, monkey-child from man.

But neither could survive the other's loss.
Without his monkey
the humble organ grinder hungered
and hunger artists never prospered
on the Czech-side streets of Prague.
The monkey had no leash or tin cup
as he wandered loose and lonely
the Jewish-German streets of Prague.

Prancing monkey, humble man,
be reconciled here. Come. Shake hands.
Come one, come all, come shoppers, tourists, skinheads,
come see the monkey do his dance again.
Come Opa, Oma, Muti, Vati,
bring Franz and Franz's pink-cheeked sister,
bring the family to the fun.
Listen to the merry music.
Feed the monkey's cup with coin—
for art's sake no one here need hunger
on the cobbled streets of Prague.

The organ grinder vows, good citizens,
if tanks should ever roll again
through the ravaged streets of Prague,
he'll repay you, though it cost him dear.
He'll kill his little monkey,
hoist it on a flagpole in the market,
then stew it up in bite-sized bits.
He'll cry for his beloved monkey
and say to you, "Here. Take and eat.
Eat of my monkey-meat"
on the streets of Prague.

The First Coming

For Chrissake how could we know right off
they weren't gods or space-aliens perched
on these winged horses cruising
into four-point landings on the Big Bear
parking lot? Then I thought
hey, April Fools' Day, quite a trick
trying to fool us, wearing these shiny
leaves strung into haloes from some tree farm.
Once they got their feet out of the stirrups
onto solid blacktop they claimed they was
"unacknowledged legislators"—Christ,
I thought, what kind of yahoos prexy deals with
back in Washington? And *here*?
By then the cops had rolled in, whining
sirens, screeching brakes, trying to make sense
of their speechifying. Which wasn't easy, seeing
they talked like they was chewing dictionaries
and spitting fancy words globbed into weird
comparisons. Yet they could speak good
central Ohio English too,
which made us suspicion they was spies
making some "raid on the inarticulate,"
like they said, and us the ones being raided.
Then they told the real whopper—
that they was flyers sent to ballyhoo
a "National Poetry Month," as if
poetry don't need to rhyme!
At long last they all jumped back on their horses.
"High-ho, Pegasus, away!" one yelled,
and away they all flew, leaving our street-cleaners
with the smelly work. Where next? I wondered—
a whole month of this horse shit.

Sunday Afternoon on Grande Jatte Island

That's my great grandmother painted on the wall,
looking as if she'd twirled a parasol
her whole young life, she preens so la-di-da,
all colored dots and splotches in her bourgeois
finery, the little seamstress! That
stiff gentleman at her right arm, whose hat
stovepipes above hers, is the neighborhood
butcher's apprentice whom she deems not good
enough for her pretensions, though he's dressed
to match all others in their Sunday best.

Both he and my great grandmother have fixed
themselves in the style of 1886.
Sunlight prisms off well-shaven lawn,
sparkles the water, casting cool shades on
those city folk self-consciously at ease
who pose there, upright as the background trees.
All over Paris artists' brushwork thrives
on swimmers, yachtsmen, strollers, hostess wives,
picnickers, dancers bathed in the new light
that glorifies their leisure or what might
become their myth of leisure.
                              My great
grandmother might have been drab Jane, her fate
not to be spotted by a Georges Seurat,
not to know Paris fashions, not to draw
her needles through whole cloth. She might have been
a peasant wasting toward oblivion
or one smudged face in a group photograph
of immigrants being herded from their craft
at Ellis Island. She'll not sink so low—
that's my great grandmother from head to toe
properly graced in the right foreground. She's
proud of her poise before those upright trees,
proud of her stitched skirt and full bustle, proud
of being the foremost figure in that crowd
of Sunday strollers—she, a refugee
from sweatshop piecework on her one day free—
proud of the class her promenade displays
and of her own designs, *her trompe l'oeil*.

Chamber Music, in Several Movements

A POET'S CHAMBER FILLED WITH GRIEF,
NOT VISITORS, the *Times* saw fit to print.
One visitor, head bowed, with back
turned to the camera, peers beneath her shawl
through a tall window
toward St. Petersburg—the Leningrad
of recent decades, jewel of Czarist Russia,
home and prison of the poet
Anna Akhmatova.
              She lived
alone, in house arrest here, through the worst
of Stalin's terror—Dante, Shakespeare,
Pushkin and the bible, with a desk
and bed her only furnishings. She lived
to tell about the purges, her first husband
shot as a counter-revolutionary,
Osip Mandelstam and other writer-friends
sent to death-camps in Siberia.

She lived by memorizing all her poems,
burning the paper they'd been written on—
"Hands, matches, ashtray,
a ritual beautiful and bitter,"
her biographer recalls.

Chamber music—
arpeggios, glissandos, obbligatos,
a grand piano's dark sheen glows
from mirrored chandeliers, a world-renowned
performer bends above the keyboard, gowned
women and men in evening dress subdue
their *tete-a-tetes* to pay a due
respect to culture and the cause
of art, for which they gather. Warm applause
mingles with aromas of glazed ham,
crabmeat soufflé, spiced pears, assorted flans.
Carved from a single block of ice, a swan
graces the champagne punch it floats upon,
the source of compliments and mutual toasts
amid the acronym-rich boasting.
Later, a noted poet will declaim

some early protest verse, then change
to elegaic land and cityscapes.

There, where she burned her poems
into mind, she lived
from shortly after Dostoyevsky's death
through both of Russia's revolutions,
two world wars, the siege of Leningrad,
Stalin's reign of terror. Yet
this room, museum for her,
one of her country's greatest poets,
attracts few visitors.

                  The hour grows late.
An aging broker will think *Tuscany*
and its munificent di Medici's.
Connoisseur of verbal images,
a software CEO, because
of tax concerns, will reckon it worthwhile
to patronize two journals in grand style.
The swan will glisten in its curve-necked bending,
a sculpted work of art *diminuendo*,
watering the punch.

Perhaps the woman at the window
recalls those years Akhmatova recorded,
committing poems, her crimes against the state,
to memory. Perhaps this woman sees
the lindens that Akhmatova so loved
and often sketched in poems, but feels
the emptiness around her, feels a change
in what had been their city—
too brisk for people to visit a dead
poet's room, or to be plagued
by painful recollections.

What fills this chamber now? A sorrow
for those commemorated by the poet?
The visitor's? Or for the moment ours,
who know how fragile memories can be?

Weight-Bearing Effigies

I.
Modigliani calls his plump-sketched forms
caryatids—in Greek temples
those draped, full-breasted female figures
bearing the weight of architrave and frieze,
pillars of the moon-goddess worship.

Disrobed, they lounge like bored young housewives
in their creamy-fleshed modernity. Breast,
belly and buttocks curve what once displayed
the upright lines of Grecian architect.
Even their faces round into their bodies,
blank, passionless, as unaware
of their own carnal beauty
as any other nude mound
or protuberance below
their languorously arching necks.

Look upon them as you will—
the absence in their faces
tempts your own reading. Yet whatever burden
you would have their female bodies carry,
it is pure physicality they bear.

II.
White as the wife of Lot, her statue leans
imploring toward the salt-surge, marble
stretching above the tide-line
as if young life stood to be restored,
that of the girl lost years ago
to the swell and crash and backward suck of waves.

Peace, says her effigy's mute pallor,
peace to those who grieved
or wept in anger, questioning.
Peace is the cooling, dense, smooth touch
of outstretched marble, the moon-drugged tide
horizon-prone, the ironwoods' gray-green
droopings behind her as she bends
her wide blank eyes upon the sea's calm.

O pray that she maintain the peace
of graven, weather-burnished monuments
before the wind and storm-tides rise and send
wave after wave against her stone-carved pose.

III.
Usually you see such small shrines
next to the road, not off the main trail
in dank vegetation near the Rhine.
Earth-bared mound, homemade wooden cross,
withered wreath and framed photograph—
traffic victims don't meet death
in the willow-brush of a low-banked river.

We kneel to read the short inscription:
HIER STARB PETRA. Petra—who?
What happened? Then we see
her picture—Petra, child who died here,
four years old at most, her child's face
dimpled, open to full exposure,
the clipped-out article beneath her smile
advising to beware of strangers.

Close by, almost out of sight,
barges toil upstream, low in the water,
the Rhine's accustomed traffic, slowed
only by cargo-weight, their mournful
drawn-out horns shivering the willows
where we stand, the small shrine
next to nothing on its moist earth.

IV
Modigliani used his art to show
that bodies bear their own messages
in bronze or marble, line, paint, weight, or gesture,
or in their haunting absence. Think of faces
in the many Pietas—
Mary's is sometimes hooded. Does she hide
a calm half-smile, a gaze of full
possession as she mothers the gaunt Christ-corpse
laid across her lap? Look rather at her robed
sloped shoulders and the angle of her head,
the bend of her back, the hands, the heavy folds
of cloth below her knees. An aged maternal

body bestows its catholic sorrow,
whatever face it wears, its pity brooding
over the weight of mortal flesh.

About the Author

Born in the Buckeye State, John N. Miller lived in various communities in Hawaii from 1937 until 1951, when he graduated from Punahou School in Honolulu. As a first-year undergraduate at Denison University in Granville, Ohio, he took two writing courses from Paul L. Bennett, a man who became his guide and mentor in poetry, and a lifelong friend for the next 50 years. At Stanford, while earning his MA and Ph.D. degrees, he worked under Yvor Winters in poetry. Later, he returned to his undergraduate alma mater, where he taught literature and creative writing for 35 years before retiring in 1997.

He and his German-born wife, Ilse Winter, now live in a Kendal retirement community in Lexington, Virginia, but frequently travel both to Hawaii and to Europe.

**Also available
from Fine Tooth Press:**

Fiction

Trespass by Craig Wolf
Trickster Tales by JP Briggs
A Poet's Guide to Divorce by David Breedan
Desperate Straits by Esther Schrader
Hardboiled Egg by Oscar De Los Santos
Darkscapes by Steven Wedel
Border Canto Trilogy (Book I) by Chuck Etheridge
Pressure Points by Craig Wolf
The Massabesic Murders by Gypsey Teague
To Beat a Dead Horse by Bill Campbell
White River by Will Bless

Non-Fiction

Spirits of Texas and New England by Oscar De Los Santos
*The New Goddess: Transgendered Women in the Twenty-First
Century* edited by Gypsey Teague
Breakout by L.R. Wright
*Scenes from an Ordinary Life: Getting Naked to Explore
a Writer's Process and Possibilities* by Lou Orfanella

Poetry

the last miles by J.D. Scrimgeour
Composite Sketches by Lou Orfanella
Balloons Over Stockholm by James R. Scrimgeour
typical girl by Donna Kuhn

In the Works:

Reel Rebels edited by Oscar De Los Santos
Street Angel by Martha Marinara

For more information about these and other titles, as well as
author bios, interviews and more, visit us on the web at:
http://www.finetoothpress.com

Printed in the United States
47802LVS00005B/127-138